COLE'S COOKING COMPANION SERIES

ITALIAN LOW-FAT

COLE GROUP

Both U.S. and metric units are provided for all recipes in this book. Ingredients are listed with U.S. units on the left and metric units on the right. The metric quantities have been rounded for ease of use; as a result, in some recipes there may be a slight difference (approximately ½ ounce or 15 grams) between the portion sizes for the two types of measurements.

Front cover photograph: Kevin Sanchez
Nutritional Analysis: Master Cook II, Arion Software Inc.

Although every effort has been made at the time of publication to guarantee the accuracy of information sources and technical data, readers must assume responsibility for selection and use of suppliers and supplies.

Cole Group, Cole colophon, and Cole's Cooking Companion are trademarks of Cole Publishing Group, Inc.

Cole Publishing Group, Inc.
1330 N. Dutton Ave., Suite 103
Santa Rosa, CA 95401
(800) 959-2717 (707) 526-2682
FAX (707) 526-2687

Printed in Hong Kong

G   F   E   D   C   B   A
1   0   9   8   7   6   5

ISBN 1-56426-814-4

Library of Congress Catalog Card Number 95-38718

Distributed to the book trade by Publishers Group West

Cole books are available for quantity purchases for sales promotions, premiums, fund-raising, or educational use. For more information on *Low-Fat Italian* or other Cole's Cooking Companion books, please write or call the publisher.

CONTENTS

Buon Gusto!

*H*omemade *pasta* tossed with vine-ripened tomatoes (*pomodori*) . . . Ring-sized dumplings floating in savory broth (*tortellini in brodo*) . . . Fresh seafood (*frutti di mare*) and fish (*pesce*) . . . Roast chicken with herbs (*pollo arrosto con aromi*) . . . Subtly sweet ices (*sorbetti*) . . . Crisp "twice-baked" cookies (*biscotti*) with espresso or sweet wine . . . Explore all the vibrant flavors of the Italian table in *Low-Fat Italian.*

THE ITALIAN TABLE

The robust flavors and aromas of the Italian table are for millions of people one of life's greatest pleasures. The traditional mid-day or evening meal (*pranzo*) in Italy, whether formal or informal, follows a pattern that seldom varies: a series of small courses—usually no more than three (special occasions call for more). Before the meal there might be an *aperitivo* (see page 19), perhaps a glass of dry vermouth or a dash of bitters over club soda, and an *antipasto* (literally "before the meal") such as marinated vegetables or seafood with a bit of bread.

The traditional first course (*primo piatto*) might consist of a rice or pasta dish at lunch or soup at supper. The second course (*secondo piatto*) typically is fish, poultry, or meat, accompanied or followed by a simple salad of raw or lightly cooked greens or a side dish of vegetables.

Except on holidays and other special occasions, Italian meals rarely include rich desserts. Fresh fruit, perhaps with a bit of cheese, or simple fruit desserts are far more common for meals at home than are elaborate sweets. Afterwards, strong coffee or espresso is served separately, away from the table.

THE HEALTHY ITALIAN KITCHEN

A collection of regional cooking styles emphasizing a variety of local ingredients, Italian cooking is as diverse as the geography and climate of *Italia*. Granted, a cuisine of such enormous diversity includes a number of traditional dishes that may seem too "rich" (in fat, cholesterol, and calories) to be part of a contemporary approach to healthy eating. But there's another side to this diverse fare, as *Low-Fat Italian* demonstrates. Like countless other health-conscious lovers of good Italian cooking, you're about to rediscover that "low-fat" doesn't have to mean "flavorless and boring."

The recipes and techniques in *Low-Fat Italian* are designed to help you prepare delectable foods worthy of the Italian table while keeping fat, cholesterol, and calories to a minimum. To reproduce the authentic flavors of *cucina Italiana,* you'll want to stock your pantry and refrigerator with some of the staples found in every health-wise Italian kitchen. Look for these items in supermarkets and specialty food stores:

Arborio rice, grown in northern Italy's Po Valley, is the preferred variety of rice for making the flavorful, slow-cooked Italian specialty known as *risotto.*

Balsamic vinegar is an aromatic aged vinegar made from Italian red wine. The vinegar imparts a distinctive mellow flavor to salads, vegetable dishes, and sauces.

Italian parsley is a flat-leaf parsley with a more pungent flavor than the curly-leaf variety commonly used as garnish.

Mushrooms, especially wild varieties such as *porcini,* lend aroma and earthy flavor to Italian dishes.

Olive oil (in small amounts) is a staple of healthy Italian cooking (see page 27). Reserve your best-quality extra virgin olive oil for salads; a less expensive grade is acceptable for sautéing and other uses that call for heating the oil.

Polenta is coarsely ground yellow cornmeal used in a variety of northern Italian dishes.

Semolina is an ivory-colored flour ground from high-protein durum wheat. Available in coarse or fine grinds, it is used in pasta and in some Italian breads.

Tomato paste, a concentrated form of tomato purée available canned or in tubes, adds intense tomato flavor to sauces and other dishes.

ABOUT THE RECIPES AND TECHNIQUES

The pace of contemporary life in the United States and elsewhere often demands more flexibility than is feasible with the traditional Italian meal, as gracious as it is. Consequently, the recipes in this book are arranged according to conventional categories: starters (appetizers and first courses); pasta, pizza, and breads; meat, poultry, and fish; and desserts and pick-me-ups. Some vegetarian dishes are included.

The recipes and techniques in *Low-Fat Italian* are compatible with a sound approach to nutrition. Each recipe includes nutritional data indicating the calories, fat, percentage of calories from fat, and cholesterol contained in the serving size indicated. Optional ingredients and inexact quantities of foods for garnishing are not included in the nutritional values.

Current dietary recommendations generally encourage reducing fat intake to an average of no more than 30 percent of the *total* number of calories consumed *daily,* with 10 percent (or less) derived from saturated fat. Emphasizing fresh produce and

other nutritious ingredients that are low in calories, dietary cholesterol, and saturated fats, most of the recipes in this book contain less than 30 percent fat; a very few are slightly higher. Following a healthy lifestyle doesn't have to preclude occasionally enjoying dishes that contain slightly more than 30 percent fat; simply choose the other foods you eat with an eye to keeping your daily average fat intake at 30 percent (or below) of the total calories you consume.

Low-Fat Italian also features healthful cooking techniques such as steaming, poaching, low-fat sautéing, baking, and grilling. Knowing how to create a variety of flavorful dishes from nutritious ingredients, using healthful cooking techniques, will add to your enjoyment of good Italian food. *Buon appetito!*

Giardiniera

These marinated vegetables are a popular item in Italian delicatessens. A large widemouthed jar allows the beauty of the vegetables to be seen easily.

2 cups	red wine vinegar	500 ml
2 tbl	olive oil	2 tbl
2 tbl	sugar	2 tbl
2 tbl	chopped Italian parsley	2 tbl
1 tsp	salt	1 tsp
3 tsp	chopped basil	3 tsp
1½ tsp	chopped oregano	1½ tsp
½ tsp	freshly ground black pepper	½ tsp
2 cloves	garlic, minced	2 cloves
2½ cups	broccoli florets	600 ml
2½ cups	cauliflower florets	600 ml
2	carrots, peeled, and cut into ½-inch (1.25-cm) pieces	2
2	red bell peppers, cored, seeded, and cut into 1-inch (2.5-cm) pieces	2
2 cups	whole mushrooms, cleaned	500 ml
2 tbl	lemon juice	2 tbl

1. In a large saucepan combine vinegar, oil, sugar, parsley, salt, basil, oregano, black pepper, and garlic. Over high heat bring mixture to a boil.

2. Add broccoli, cauliflower, and carrots. Again bring mixture to boiling and add bell pepper and mushrooms. Remove mixture from heat and cool to room temperature, then stir in lemon juice. Pour into a widemouthed 2-quart (1.8-l) jar, cover, and refrigerate up to 7 days.

Serves 12.
Each serving: cal 62, fat 3 g, cal from fat 31%, chol 0 mg

SICILIAN TOMATO SPREAD WITH SCAMPI

Traditional Italian cooks used to make tomato paste by leaving tomato sauce in the sun to dry out. The resultant paste was enjoyed as a snack, spread on bread. This updated version is disarmingly simple—tomato paste spruced up with garlic and fresh herbs—but remarkably tasty when slathered on bread sticks, scampi (prawns), or a rustic loaf of bread (pane). It will keep under oil, refrigerated, for a week.

½ cup	tomato paste	125 ml
1 tbl	red wine vinegar	1 tbl
1 tbl	olive oil	1 tbl
½ tsp	chopped thyme	½ tsp
1 clove	garlic, minced	1 clove
1 pound	cooked jumbo prawns	450 g
as needed	lemon slices, for garnish	as needed

1. Combine all ingredients except prawns and lemon slices thoroughly. Spoon into a small serving bowl or pack into a small crock, cover with a thin film of olive oil, and refrigerate for up to a week.

2. To serve, place bowl of tomato spread in center of platter. Arrange prawns and lemon slices around the bowl of tomato spread and serve at once.

Serves 8.
Each serving: cal 90, fat 3 g, cal from fat 28%, chol 86 mg

STARTERS

A sweet and tangy salad of roasted peppers, a mélange of summer vegetables in a pesto-enriched broth, savory sautéed onions tucked between layers of zucchini and tomatoes—succulent dishes like these start a meal off delectably without adding unwanted fat, cholesterol, and calories. From Zuppa Bolognese (see page 27) to Insalata Mista (see page 20), this section offers enough appetizers and first courses to please anyone who fancies healthy Italian cuisine.

RECIPES AND TECHNIQUES FOR LOW-FAT ITALIAN CUISINE

*I*n the following chapters you'll find specialties from every region and corner of Italy, traditional dishes as well as innovative contemporary variations of Italian classics— all of them streamlined for health-minded cooks concerned about reducing dietary fat and cholesterol, as well as calories. From *antipasto* to *sorbetto, biscotti* to *ravioli*—all your favorite healthy Italian fare is here.

TUSCAN WHITE BEAN AND TUNA SALAD

Serve this delectable and nutritious combination with a peasant-style Italian bread as an appetizer or first course.

2 cans (15 oz each)	white cannellini beans	2 cans (430 g each)
1	red onion, minced	1
1 clove	garlic, minced	1 clove
2 cans (6 oz each)	tuna, packed in water	2 cans (170 g each)
1 tbl	olive oil	1 tbl
3 tbl	red wine vinegar	3 tbl
4 tbl	minced Italian parsley	4 tbl
4 tbl	dried sage	4 tbl
1 tsp	salt	1 tsp
½ tsp	freshly ground black pepper	½ tsp
4 tbl	minced chives, for garnish	4 tbl

1. In a large bowl gently stir together all ingredients except chives.

2. Marinate 4–48 hours in the refrigerator to let flavors meld. Serve at room temperature garnished with chives.

Serves 8.
Each serving: cal 226, fat 3 g, cal from fat 10%, chol 13 mg

PIEDMONT PEPPER SALAD

This colorful roasted pepper salad (see photo on page 4) can be made up to one day ahead and stored in the refrigerator, covered. Serve it at room temperature for the best flavor.

8	roasted red bell peppers (see page 21), or a combination of red, green, and yellow peppers	8
½ tbl	olive oil	½ tbl
1 tbl	balsamic vinegar	1 tbl
1 tbl each	finely chopped Italian parsley and basil	1 tbl each
1 clove	garlic, minced	1 clove

1. Cut roasted peppers in half, holding them over a bowl to catch juice. Reserve juice. Remove seeds and stems. Tear or cut peppers lengthwise into strips about 1 inch (2.5 cm) wide. Place in a serving bowl and set aside.

2. In a small bowl whisk together reserved pepper juice, olive oil, vinegar, herbs, and garlic. Pour over peppers.

3. Serve immediately or marinate at room temperature several hours.

Serves 8.
Each serving: cal 29, fat 1 g, cal from fat 28%, chol 0 mg

PASTA SALAD WITH PEAS AND PROSCIUTTO

A bit of prosciutto adds flavor and color to this recipe.

1 tsp	olive oil	1 tsp
¼ cup	dry sherry	60 ml
½ cup	sliced red bell pepper	125 ml
1 tbl	minced garlic	1 tbl
⅓ cup	cooked prosciutto ham, fat trimmed off	85 ml
¼ cup	chopped basil	60 ml
2 tbl	chopped Italian parsley	2 tbl
1 tsp	dried thyme	1 tsp
1 cup	fresh peas	250 ml
4 cups	cooked small pasta shells	900 ml
2 tbl	freshly grated Parmesan cheese	2 tbl

1. Into a skillet over medium-high heat pour oil and sherry and sauté bell pepper and garlic for 3 minutes.

2. Add remaining ingredients and cook, stirring, until peas turn bright green (about 1 minute). Serve hot or cold.

Serves 4.
Each serving: cal 311, fat 5 g, cal from fat 14%, chol 15 mg

THE ITALIAN APERITIVO

A classic way to begin a traditional Italian meal is with an aperitivo—typically a glass of spirits intended to awaken the palate. Popular Italian aperitivi such as cynar, dry vermouth, or bitters and club soda have only about 100 calories for a 3½-oz (150-ml) glass, making them a good alternative to high-calorie beer or wine. Most have a bitter but refreshing taste, the better to pique the appetite without sending it out of control.

Insalata Mista

The classic Italian mixed green salad ("insalata mista") calls for the freshest greens and other seasonal ingredients (see photo on page 11). Look for a market that takes good care of its produce and select whatever is freshest and in season.

Carefully wash greens and dry thoroughly. Do not break or chop them. Wrap greens in damp paper towels, place in crisper drawer, and refrigerate until serving time. Chill salad bowl and plates.

To serve, tear greens into large pieces or leave whole. Toss greens with your favorite low-fat vinaigrette, using wooden utensils if possible; metal utensils bruise the leaves, and the heat of your hands can wilt this delicate salad. Divide among salad plates or serve from the bowl. Offer a pepper mill at the table.

Good choices for Insalata Mista include

- *hearts of romaine lettuce*
- *butterhead lettuce*
- *red-leaf lettuce*
- *limestone lettuce*
- *Belgian endive*
- *arugula*
- *radicchio*
- *purple kale*

- *dandelion greens*
- *tender radish tops*
- *young sorrel leaves*
- *oregano leaves*
- *whole small basil leaves*
- *thyme flowers*
- *chive flowers*

ROASTING PEPPERS

Throughout Italy, cooks roast sweet peppers and serve them as a salad or add them to a variety of dishes. A few strips of roasted peppers add vibrant color and flavor to any meal. Although bottled roasted peppers are available in most markets, preparing them yourself is simple and far more economical.

- *If possible, remove a burner grid from gas stove, or heat broiler of electric range.*

- *With a gas stove: Using long tongs or a long roasting fork, hold peppers (one at a time) directly over high flame, turning peppers until all sides are blistered and blackened. With an electric range: Place peppers close to heat source and broil, turning frequently, until blackened.*

- *Place blackened peppers in a paper bag. Seal top of bag and let stand for 10 minutes after sealing.*

- *Remove peppers from bag and, under cold running water, peel skin away with fingers (aided by a small, sharp knife, if necessary). Trim away stems, seeds, and heavy veins and slice or tear into strips.*

SCALLOP-RED PEPPER SALAD

A tangy vinaigrette adds zest to steamed scallops.

1 tbl	lemon juice	1 tbl
1 tbl	balsamic vinegar	1 tbl
as needed	olive oil	as needed
2	red bell peppers, cored and cut in thin strips	2
as needed	salt	as needed
12 leaves	leaf lettuce	12 leaves
¾ lb	sea scallops	350 g
as needed	freshly ground black pepper	as needed
½ cup	pitted black olives	125 ml

1. In a small bowl combine lemon juice, vinegar, and 2 teaspoons of oil. Set aside.

2. Heat 1 teaspoon of oil in a frying pan over medium-low heat. Add bell pepper and a pinch of salt and sauté until barely tender (about 3 minutes). Transfer peppers to a plate and set aside.

3. Arrange lettuce on a serving platter. Rinse scallops and pat dry with paper towels.

4. Bring 1 inch (2.5 cm) of water to a boil in base of steamer. Boiling water should not reach holes in top part of steamer. Season scallops with salt and pepper. Arrange them in one layer in steamer top and set above boiling water. Cover and steam over high heat until tender (about 3 minutes). Drain on paper towels.

5. Arrange warm scallops over lettuce. Whisk lemon juice mixture and spoon over scallops. Arrange peppers and olives around scallops. Serve immediately.

Serves 4.
Each serving: cal 131, fat 5 g, cal from fat 32%, chol 28 mg

Minestrone con Aromi

Fresh vegetables, herbs (aromi), and fusilli pasta float in a delicate broth to create a low-fat soup perfect for summer evenings.

1 tbl	olive oil	1 tbl
1	onion, diced	1
2 stalks	celery, diced	2 stalks
4 cloves	garlic, diced	4 cloves
2	carrots, peeled and cut into ½-inch (1.25-cm) sections	2
8	plum tomatoes, diced	8
½ cup	minced Italian parsley	125 ml
3 tbl each	minced basil and oregano	3 tbl each
2	bay leaves	2
4 tsp	salt	4 tsp
1 tsp	freshly ground black pepper	1 tsp
3 cups	cooked, small white beans	700 ml
½ lb	fusilli	225 g
½ lb	diced green beans	225 g
2	zucchini, diced	2
as needed	grated Parmesan cheese, for garnish	as needed

1. In a skillet over low flame heat oil. Add onion, celery, and garlic and sauté for 6 minutes.

2. Bring 12 cups (2.7 l) water to a boil and add to onion mixture. Add carrots, tomatoes, herbs, salt, pepper, white beans, and pasta. Reduce heat to medium, and simmer for 20 minutes. Add green beans and cook for 5 minutes. Add zucchini and cook for 3 minutes more. Ladle into soup bowls and sprinkle with Parmesan cheese.

Serves 12.
Each serving: cal 205, fat 4 g, cal from fat 15%, chol 4 mg

ZUPPA DI ZUCCA

Nutritious and remarkably satisfying, this Sicilian soup is best made with small sugar pumpkins.

1 tbl	olive oil	1 tbl
3	carrots, peeled and diced	3
2½ cups	diced red onion	600 ml
1	leek, washed and sliced	1
1	parsnip, peeled and diced	1
1 lb	pumpkin, peeled and cubed	450 g
4 cups	Chicken Stock (see page 30)	900 ml
2 tbl	grated lemon zest	2 tbl
3 tbl	lemon juice	3 tbl
1 tsp	dried oregano	1 tsp
¼ tsp	hot-pepper flakes	¼ tsp
1 cup	skim milk	250 ml
to taste	salt and freshly ground black pepper	to taste
3 tbl	minced Italian parsley	3 tbl

1. Into a stockpot over moderate heat pour oil. Add carrots, onion, leek, and parsnip; sauté 5 minutes. Add pumpkin, stock, 2 teaspoons of the lemon zest, lemon juice, oregano, and pepper flakes. Cover and simmer until pumpkin is tender. Cool slightly.

2. Transfer mixture in batches to a blender and blend, adding some of the milk to each batch to facilitate blending. Return soup to stockpot. Season to taste with salt and pepper. Blend remaining lemon zest with parsley. Reheat soup and serve garnished with parsley-lemon zest mixture.

Serves 10.
Each serving: cal 92, fat 2 g, cal from fat 21%, chol 0 mg

ZUPPA BOLOGNESE

Fresh chard adds color and flavor to this soup.

2 bunches	green or red chard	2 bunches
1 tbl	olive oil	1 tbl
¼ cup	minced onion	60 ml
3 cups	Chicken Stock (see page 30)	700 ml
½ cup	Arborio rice	125 ml
⅓ cup	julienned basil leaves	85 ml
as needed	freshly grated Parmesan cheese	as needed

1. Wash chard; remove stems and cut them into dice. Blanch leaves in salted boiling water for 10–15 seconds, then transfer to ice water; drain, squeeze dry, and chop coarsely. Set aside. Blanch stems in the same boiling water and refresh in ice water; drain and dry.

2. Heat oil in a stockpot over moderate heat. Add onion and sauté until translucent (about 3–5 minutes). Add chard stems and stir to coat with oil. Add stock and rice and bring to a simmer. Cover and simmer gently 15 minutes or until rice is just cooked. Add chopped chard leaves and heat through.

3. To serve, garnish with basil and Parmesan cheese.

Serves 8.
Each serving: cal 76, fat 2 g, cal from fat 28%, chol 0 mg

A LITTLE GOES A LONG WAY

The highest grade of olive oil, extra virgin, is pressed from olives that have not been subjected to chemical treatments of any kind. The superior flavor of extra virgin olive oil makes it the perfect choice for health-conscious cooks because only a small amount is needed to significantly improve the taste of any dish.

LIGURIAN PESTO SOUP

A region in northern Italy, Liguria is known for its sweet, aromatic basil the prime ingredient in the pungent sauce known as pesto.

Pesto

2 cloves	garlic, minced	2 cloves
1 cup	chopped basil leaves	250 ml
¼ cup	finely chopped walnuts	60 ml
2 tbl	freshly grated Parmesan cheese	2 tbl
1 tsp	olive oil	1 tsp
⅓ cup	sliced onion	85 ml
½ cup	diced red potato	125 ml
½ cup	sliced green beans	125 ml
½ cup	sliced zucchini	125 ml
¼ cup	chopped celery leaves	60 ml
½ cup	peeled and chopped tomato	125 ml
1 cup	cooked navy beans	250 ml
⅛ tsp	saffron	⅛ tsp
½ tsp	freshly ground black pepper	½ tsp
4 cups	Chicken Stock (see page 30)	900 ml
2 tbl	tomato paste	2 tbl
to taste	salt	to taste

1. In a blender combine garlic, basil, walnuts and cheese, and purée. Set Pesto aside.

2. Into a stockpot over medium heat pour oil; add onion and sauté over medium heat until onion is soft. Add remaining ingredients except for tomato paste and salt. Bring to a boil, cover, and simmer 35 minutes, stirring occasionally. Stir in tomato paste and pesto; season to taste with salt.

Serves 6.
Each serving: cal 166, fat 6 g, cal from fat 30%, chol 1 mg

LOW-FAT STOCKS

Nothing from a can or foil packet compares to the robust flavor of a homemade stock. Another advantage to preparing your own stock is that you can remove the fat in one simple step. Allow stock to chill for 2 hours or long enough for the fat to separate and rise to the top. Remove fat with a spoon and discard. Regardless of the base, do not boil stock. Boiling releases acids that may give stock a bitter taste. Both recipes yield 4 cups (900 ml). Store defatted stock up to a week in the refrigerator or for two months in the freezer.

Beef Stock

1 tsp	olive or canola oil	1 tsp
3 lb	beef bones	1.4 kg
1 stalk	celery	1 stalk
1	onion	1
1	bay leaf	1
1	carrot	1

To a stockpot over high heat add oil and brown the bones. Then add remaining ingredients and water to cover. Simmer 3 hours and strain. Cool, then chill before removing fat.

Chicken Stock

2 lb	chicken backs and necks	900 g
1 stalk	celery	1 stalk
1	onion, quartered	1
1	bay leaf	1
1	carrot	1

In a stockpot combine chicken, celery, onion, bay leaf, and carrot. Add water to cover. Simmer over low heat 1½ hours and strain. Cool, then chill before removing fat.

Tortellini in Brodo

Traditionally made at home and filled by hand, tortellini are synonymous with Bologna, an Italian city famous for its fresh homemade pasta. Use good-quality fresh or frozen tortellini and, if you like, add fresh peas or asparagus tips to the soup for an easy variation.

8 cups	Beef Stock (see page 30)	1.8 l
3 tbl	chopped basil	3 tbl
10 oz	fresh or frozen tortellini	285 g
1 tbl	freshly grated Parmesan cheese	1 tbl

1. Bring stock to a boil over medium-high heat; add basil and tortellini. Return soup to a boil, reduce heat to simmer, and cook until tortellini are tender (about 10 minutes, or according to package instructions).

2. Divide stock and tortellini among 6 shallow soup bowls, sprinkling each serving with Parmesan cheese.

Serves 6.
Each serving: cal 104, fat 4 g, cal from fat 35%, chol 62 mg

CECI AL SALTO

Chilled and tossed with a low-fat vinaigrette, this chick-pea (ceci) sauté (al salto) becomes a delicious salad.

1 bunch	broccoli	1 bunch
2 sprigs	rosemary	2 sprigs
1 tbl	olive oil	1 tbl
1	onion, diced	1
2 cloves	garlic, minced	2 cloves
1	plum tomato, finely diced	1
3½ cups	cooked chick-peas	800 ml
½ tsp	salt	½ tsp
¼ tsp	freshly ground black pepper	¼ tsp
1 tbl	balsamic vinegar	1 tbl

1. Cut broccoli into bite-sized pieces. Strip leaves from sprigs of rosemary. Discard sprigs.

2. Into a medium saucepan over medium heat pour oil. Add onion and garlic, and sauté 5–6 minutes. Add broccoli, tomato, and chick-peas. Stir to combine and season with rosemary, salt, pepper, and vinegar. Cook over low heat for 10 minutes to heat through. Serve warm or at room temperature.

Serves 6.
Each serving: cal 194, fat 5 g, cal from fat 22%, chol 0 mg

THE VERSATILE SUMMER SQUASH

Given its prolific nature in the vegetable garden, it's good to know that zucchini can be enjoyed in so many ways. High in potassium and vitamin A and low in fat, this versatile squash can be sliced into salads, grated into muffins, pickled, sautéed, puréed, baked, grilled, or hollowed out and stuffed with rice and herbs.

POMODORI CON ZUCCHINE

Italy in the height of summer means an abundance of vine-ripened tomatoes and zucchini—and lots of deliciously rustic dishes like this one.

1½ tsp	olive oil	1½ tsp
1	red onion, sliced into thick rounds	1
3 cloves	garlic, minced	3 cloves
4	zucchini, sliced ½ inch (1.25 cm) thick	4
3	plum tomatoes, sliced	3
½ tsp	salt	½ tsp
¼ tsp	freshly ground black pepper	¼ tsp
1 tbl	dried thyme	1 tbl
3 tbl	Gruyère cheese, grated	3 tbl

1. Preheat oven to 350°F (175°C). Into a large skillet over medium heat pour oil. Sauté onion and garlic until translucent (5–8 minutes).

2. Place zucchini slices on edge along the perimeter of an 8-inch (20-cm) round baking dish (cut edge against the side of the dish). Place tomato slices on edge against the zucchini, spooning in some of the sautéed onion-garlic mixture to hold the vegetables upright. Repeat with remaining zucchini, tomato, and onion-garlic mixture to form alternating rings. Place remaining vegetables in center. Sprinkle with salt, pepper, thyme, and cheese.

3. Bake for 25 minutes. Serve warm.

Serves 6.
Each serving: cal 59, fat 2 g, cal from fat 30%, chol 3 mg

POMODORI CON AROMI

Fresh Italian parsley and basil enliven this easy-to-make tomato dish. Perfect for a picnic, this dish goes well with Grilled Sicilian Chicken (see page 74) and a loaf of crusty Italian bread.

1 tsp	olive oil	1 tsp
1½ pints	cherry tomatoes, stemmed	600 ml
1½ tbl each	finely chopped Italian parsley and basil	1½ tbl each
to taste	salt and freshly ground black pepper	to taste

1. Into a large skillet over medium heat pour oil. Add tomatoes and sauté, stirring occasionally, about 2–3 minutes. Cook just until tomatoes are soft, but do not let them burst.

2. Sprinkle with herbs and toss to coat. Season to taste with salt and pepper. Serve warm or at room temperature.

Serves 6.
Each serving: cal 26, fat 1 g, cal from fat 32%, chol 0 mg

MELANZANE MEDITERRANEAN

Salt the eggplant before baking to allow the fibers to soften and better absorb the flavors of the other ingredients.

1	eggplant, sliced ½ inch (1.25 cm) thick	1
as needed	salt	as needed
1 tbl	olive oil	1 tbl
1	onion, sliced	1
2 cloves	garlic, minced	2 cloves
2	ripe tomatoes, sliced	2
3 tbl	chopped basil	3 tbl
2 tsp	dried oregano	2 tsp
½ cup	white wine	125 ml
1 cup	cooked chick-peas	250 ml
2	eggs, beaten lightly	2
2 tbl	freshly grated Parmesan cheese	2 tbl

1. Preheat oven to 300°F (150°C). Place eggplant slices on a baking tray and sprinkle with salt. Let stand for 15 minutes, then rinse salt from eggplant slices and pat dry with paper towels. Bake eggplant until easily pierced with a fork (about 10–15 minutes).

2. While eggplant is baking, heat oil in a skillet and sauté onion until soft, then add garlic, tomatoes, basil, oregano, and wine. Cook until tomatoes soften (about 10 minutes).

3. Raise temperature of oven to 350°F (175°C). Place baked eggplant in a baking dish.

4. Spread chick-peas over eggplant; top with beaten eggs. Spoon tomato mixture over eggs. Sprinkle with cheese and bake for 45 minutes. Serve hot.

Serves 4.
Each serving: cal 146, fat 6 g, cal from fat 35%, chol 72 mg

HERBS: FLAVORFUL AND FAT-FREE

Seasoning your favorite Italian dishes with fresh or dried herbs is a great way to gain fantastic flavor without adding unwanted fat. The following herbs common to Italian cooking bring out the best in a variety of foods:

Eggplant, pepper, potato, tomato *Basil, bay, garlic, marjoram, oregano, Italian parsley, rosemary, sage, thyme*

Mushrooms *Basil, bay, marjoram, oregano, Italian parsley, thyme*

Onion, garlic, leek *Basil, bay, marjoram, oregano, Italian parsley, rosemary, sage, thyme*

Summer squash and zucchini *Marjoram, oregano, Italian parsley, rosemary, thyme*

PATATE AL FORNO

Prepared in Tuscan fashion, these potato wedges are brushed with a light coating of olive oil, baked, and dusted with minced garlic and Parmesan cheese.

4	baking potatoes	4
3 tsp	olive oil	3 tsp
to taste	salt	to taste
1 tbl	finely minced garlic	1 tbl
2 tsp	freshly grated Parmesan cheese	2 tsp

1. Preheat oven to 375°F (190°C). Wash potatoes, dry well, and quarter lengthwise. In a large bowl combine 1 tablespoon water with 2 teaspoons of the oil and toss potatoes in the mixture. Arrange on a heavy baking sheet. Dust with salt and bake until well browned and cooked through (about 20 minutes).

2. When potatoes are almost tender, heat remaining olive oil in a small saucepan or skillet over moderately low heat. Add garlic and cook 1 minute, stirring constantly. Do not allow garlic to burn. Set aside.

3. Transfer potatoes to a warm serving platter; sprinkle with garlic and cheese and lightly toss to coat. Serve warm.

Serves 4.
Each serving: cal 126, fat 4 g, cal from fat 26%, chol 1 mg

Pasta, Pizza, and Breads

Few foods are as satisfying as fresh-baked bread, a plate of steaming pasta, or a hot slice of pizza. This section offers delicious versions of these Italian staples that are low in cholesterol, fat, and calories. Crunch into the cornmeal crust of Pizza con Polenta (see page 55) or sink your teeth into a slice of Focaccia (see page 56). You needn't refrain from indulging in the culinary pleasures these dishes are guaranteed to provide.

ANGEL HAIR PRIMAVERA

Delicate yet satisfying, this dish combines angel hair pasta with fresh vegetables.

¾ lb	angel hair pasta	350 g
1 lb	sugar snap peas, strings removed	450 g
1 lb	asparagus, trimmed	450 g
1 cup	sliced green beans	250 ml
½ cup	thin carrot strips	125 ml
2 tbl	olive oil	2 tbl
1 tbl	unsalted butter	1 tbl
1 cup	diced red bell pepper	250 ml
2 tbl	pine nuts, toasted	2 tbl
1 cup	shredded romaine lettuce	250 ml
2 tbl	minced chives	2 tbl
to taste	salt	to taste
4 tbl	minced Italian parsley, for garnish	4 tbl

1. Cook and drain pasta, reserving cooking water. Set cooked pasta aside and keep warm.

2. Bring reserved water to a boil. Blanch peas, asparagus, beans, and carrots separately, removing each batch to ice water as vegetables become tender but are still crisp, to stop the cooking. Drain and pat dry.

3. Heat olive oil and butter in a skillet over moderate heat. Add pepper and sauté 1 minute. Add pine nuts and sauté 1 more minute. Add blanched and drained peas, asparagus, beans, and carrots and toss until coated with oil and warmed through.

4. Place cooked pasta in a serving bowl. Add hot vegetables to pasta with lettuce and chives. Toss well and add salt to taste. Garnish with minced parsley.

Serves 4.
Each serving: cal 520, fat 14 g, cal from fat 24%, chol 8 mg

Basic Egg Dough for Pasta

Use this recipe to make traditional cut pasta shapes such as fettuccine (flat ribbons) or lasagne (broad strips), or filled pasta such as ravioli (see page 44). Replacing all or part of the unbleached flour in this recipe with semolina (see page 8) creates a firm, elastic, fine-textured dough.

Add another dimension to fresh pasta by varying the flavor. Many supermarkets carry flavored pasta, but there are advantages to making it at home. You can use the freshest ingredients and experiment with flavors until you find the perfect combination. Try adding pureéd vegetables such as cooked spinach, pumpkin, beets, or roasted red peppers (see page 21); fresh puréed garlic; or spices and seasonings such as black pepper, cayenne, cinnamon, chili powder, curry, nutmeg, or saffron. Fresh or dried chopped black olives or fresh or canned chopped hot chiles are also great complements to this recipe. Depending on which ingredients you add, it may be necessary to adjust the proportions of liquid and flour to form a dough of proper consistency.

1½ cups	unbleached flour or semolina, or a mixture	350 ml
1 tsp	salt	1 tsp
2	eggs, lightly beaten	2

Combine and mix ingredients according to instructions on opposite page.

Makes 1¼ pounds (570 g) fresh pasta, serves 4.
Each serving: cal 208, fat 3 g, cal from fat 13%, chol 106 mg

Preparing Fresh Pasta

Machines can be convenient for making pasta, but they aren't essential. With only a bowl, a fork, a rolling pin, and a knife, you can turn out professional-quality fresh pasta in 10 minutes.

2. Lightly flour work surface. Start with a third of the dough at a time. Starting from the center and moving to the edge, roll the pasta, using as few strokes as possible. If dough becomes too elastic, cover it for a few minutes with a damp cloth to prevent it from drying out. Roll out about 1/8–1/16 inch (.3-.2 cm) thick.

1. Make a well of flour blended with salt on a clean work surface. Place beaten egg in center of well. Use a fork or your fingertips to incorporate the flour into beaten egg to form a firm dough. On a flour-dusted work surface, knead dough until it is smooth and cohesive (5–8 minutes). Cover with damp cloth. Let rest for 15 minutes.

3. Lightly flour dough and roll into a jelly-roll shape. Cut by hand to desired thickness for flat shapes (such as linguine, fettuccine, or lasagne). Dry 10–15 minutes on a pasta rack before cooking (see page 47).

PREPARING RAVIOLI

Ravioli can be made with a variety of doughs and fillings (see pages 42–43 and 46). The dough should be rolled quite thin. Using a mold to form the ravioli simplifies the process but is not essential. Ravioli can be prepared a few hours ahead of serving time and spread on lightly floured baking sheets. Make sure they do not touch. Cover and refrigerate.

To freeze uncooked ravioli, place in a lock-top plastic bag and use within three months. After cooking, ravioli can be added to stock (see page 30) or sauced with Sugo di Pomodori Freschi or Sugo di Pomodoro (see pages 48 and 50) or a purchased sauce.

1. Roll pasta dough into thin sheets. Place mounds of filling, about ¾ teaspoon each, at regular intervals the length of the pasta. Brush lightly with cold water between the mounds.

2. Place another sheet of pasta over the first and use your fingers to press sheets together between the mounds of filling.

3. Cut ravioli with a pizza cutter or pastry wheel. Use a fork to crimp and seal the edges. Cook according to instructions on page 47.

BAKED ORZO

The tiny dried pasta shape known as orzo resembles grains of rice. Here it's cooked like a rice pilaf— first sautéed, then steam-baked in hot stock. Don't be fooled by the simple ingredients—this dish is a real showstopper.

1 tbl	butter	1 tbl
¼ cup	minced shallot	60 ml
1 tbl	minced garlic	1 tbl
¼ cup	minced carrot	60 ml
1 cup	orzo	250 ml
1¼ cups	hot Chicken or Beef Stock (see page 30)	300 ml
2 tbl	freshly grated Parmesan cheese	2 tbl

1. Preheat oven to 350°F (175°C). In an ovenproof skillet or casserole over low heat, melt butter. Add shallot, garlic, and carrot and cook 2 minutes, stirring. Add orzo and cook 3 minutes, stirring constantly.

2. Add stock, cover, and transfer skillet to oven. Bake 20 minutes. Uncover and stir in Parmesan with a fork. Serve immediately.

Serves 4.
Each serving: cal 143, fat 4 g, cal from fat 28%, chol 10 mg

Ravioli di Scarole

These plump little pillows from Bologna have a colorful, savory filling that's complemented by a flavorful tomato sauce (see photo on cover).

1 tbl	olive oil	1 tbl
1 tbl	butter	1 tbl
3 tbl	minced leek or onion	3 tbl
1½ tsp	minced garlic	1½ tsp
1 bunch	escarole, washed and finely shredded	1 bunch
1 tsp	dried oregano	1 tsp
2 tbl	Marsala	2 tbl
2 tbl	light whipping cream	2 tbl
¼ cup	ricotta cheese, part skim milk	60 ml
¼ cup	freshly grated mozzarella cheese, part skim milk	60 ml
to taste	salt and freshly ground black pepper	to taste
pinch	ground nutmeg	pinch
2 recipes	Basic Egg Dough (see page 42)	2 recipes
1 recipe	Sugo di Pomodoro (see page 50)	1 recipe
3 tbl	minced Italian parsley, for garnish	3 tbl
¼ cup	freshly grated Parmesan cheese	60 ml

1. To a skillet over moderate heat add oil and butter. When butter foams, add leek and garlic. Sauté gently until leek is very soft (about 15 minutes). Add escarole and oregano and sauté 2 minutes.

2. Add Marsala, turn heat up to high, and cook until Marsala is almost completely evaporated. Reduce heat to medium and add cream. Stir to combine; simmer until cream thickens into a sauce, about 2–3 minutes. Remove from heat and cool slightly. Stir in cheeses; season to taste with salt, pepper, and nutmeg. Set aside.

3. Fill ravioli according to instructions on page 44.

4. Bring a large pot of salted water to a boil. Add ravioli to boiling water a few at a time; do not crowd the pot. Ravioli will sink, then float. After they begin to float, cook 2½ minutes. Remove one and taste for doneness. With a slotted spoon, remove cooked ravioli to a warm platter and keep warm. Add remaining ravioli to boiling water in batches until all are cooked.

5. Meanwhile, reheat sauce. When all ravioli are on the platter, top with hot sauce. Garnish with parsley and Parmesan cheese.

Serves 8.
Each serving: cal 339, fat 11 g, cal from fat 28%, chol 94 mg

---

COOKING PASTA

Properly cooked pasta should offer slight resistance to the tooth (al dente), without being soft or mushy. For each pound (450 g) of pasta, bring about 4 quarts (3.6 l) of water to a rapid boil. Add a little salt, drop the pasta in all at once, stir, and cover the pot. When the water returns to a boil, uncover and boil until pasta is al dente. Fresh pasta generally cooks in 60–90 seconds; dried pasta may take 5 minutes or more, depending on its shape and age. Cook frozen pasta by dropping it directly into boiling water; do not thaw before cooking.

Drain cooked pasta in a colander, shaking to drain off excess cooking water (reserve a little of the cooking water); then pour pasta into a warm bowl. Add a little olive oil or sauce and toss. If the pasta seems too thick or dry, add a bit of the reserved cooking water to moisten. Serve immediately.

Sugo di Pomodori Freschi

For a delightful dish that makes the most of fresh tomatoes, serve this sauce over packaged or homemade pasta (see page 42). Be sure to let the finished sauce sit for 30 minutes to allow flavors to meld before serving.

3 lb	fresh vine-ripened tomatoes, peeled, seeded, and diced (see page 51)	1.4 kg
2 tbl	garlic, finely minced	2 tbl
1 tbl	olive oil	1 tbl
¼ cup	chopped basil	60 ml
2 tbl	minced Italian parsley	2 tbl
½ tsp	hot-pepper flakes	½ tsp
to taste	freshly ground black pepper	to taste
1 tbl	balsamic vinegar	1 tbl
1 tsp	salt	1 tsp

1. Combine all ingredients except salt in a large non-aluminum bowl. Stir to blend well; then let sit at room temperature for 30 minutes.

2. Just before serving, add salt to sauce.

Serves 6.
Each serving: cal 73, fat 3 g, cal from fat 33%, chol 0 mg

Sugo di Pomodoro

Substitute canned tomatoes, imported from Italy, for the fresh plum tomatoes used in this versatile sauce if vine-ripened ones are not available. This sauce is an excellent complement to fresh homemade ravioli (see page 46).

2 tsp	olive oil	2 tsp
2 tsp	butter	2 tsp
1	carrot, peeled and diced	1
2 stalks	celery, diced	2 stalks
1	onion, diced	1
2 tbl	minced garlic	2 tbl
1 tsp	flour	1 tsp
3 lb	ripe plum tomatoes, peeled, seeded, and chopped (see page 51)	1.4 kg
1 tbl	tomato paste	1 tbl
pinch	sugar	pinch
1 tsp	dried basil	1 tsp
4 sprigs	Italian parsley	4 sprigs
2 sprigs	oregano	2 sprigs
1	bay leaf	1
to taste	salt and freshly ground black pepper	to taste

1. In a large, heavy saucepan over moderate heat place oil and butter. Add carrot, celery, onion, and garlic and sauté gently for 10 minutes. Stir in flour and continue cooking 5 minutes.

2. Add remaining ingredients except salt and pepper. Simmer, partly covered, for 1 hour.

3. Remove bay leaf and herb stems. Season to taste with salt and pepper. Serve warm.

Makes 4 cups (900 ml), serves 8.
Each serving: cal 74, fat 3 g, cal from fat 31%, chol 3 mg

PREPARING TOMATOES

Tomatoes, the basis for hundreds of Italian dishes, are a delicious and nonfat source of potassium, vitamin A, and vitamin C. Select tomatoes that are fragrant and fully ripe, and keep them out of the refrigerator if you want to maintain peak flavor.

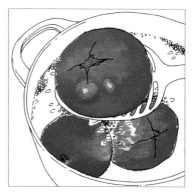

2. Put the tomatoes in a pan containing enough boiling water to cover them. After 15 seconds remove them with a slotted spoon and put them in a bowl of cold water for a few seconds.

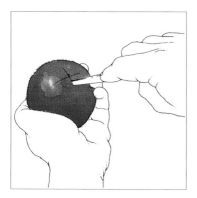

1. Use a paring knife to core the tomatoes. Turn tomatoes over and slit an X-shaped cut.

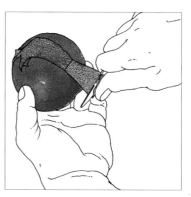

3. Remove them from the cold water and use a paring knife to pull off the skins. Halve the tomatoes horizontally with a chopping knife. Hold each half over a bowl, cut side down, and squeeze to remove the seeds, if desired. Chop the tomatoes into small pieces.

ZITI CON SALSICCE

Replacing traditional Italian sausage (salsicce) with good-quality turkey sausage reduces the fat without affecting the flavor of this simple dish.

¾ lb	turkey sausage, cut into ¾-inch (1.9-cm) pieces	350 g
1	onion, sliced thinly	1
3 cloves	garlic, minced	3 cloves
2½ lb	ripe tomatoes, peeled and coarsely chopped, (see page 51)	1.2 kg
⅓ cup	Marsala	85 ml
¼ cup	chopped basil leaves	60 ml
to taste	salt and freshly ground black pepper	to taste
8 oz	ziti	225 g

1. In a Dutch oven over medium heat brown sausage for about 5 minutes. Push sausage to side of pan. Add onion and garlic; sauté about 2 minutes. Pour off any fat in pan.

2. Add tomatoes and Marsala to pan. Cook over medium heat until sauce reduces and thickens (about 5–10 minutes).

3. Stir in basil. Season to taste with salt and pepper. Set aside and keep warm.

4. Cook ziti, following package directions. Drain. Toss pasta with sauce and serve immediately.

Serves 4.
Each serving: cal 433, fat 10 g, cal from fat 21%, chol 67 mg

PESTO-POTATO PIZZA

Roasted red potatoes and fresh pesto create a delicious pizza that's surprisingly low in fat.

2 cups	thinly sliced red-skinned new potatoes	500 ml
to taste	salt and freshly ground black pepper	to taste
½ tbl	olive oil	½ tbl
1 recipe	Pesto (see page 28)	1 recipe
1	16-inch (40-cm) unbaked pizza crust	1
2 tbl	freshly grated Parmesan cheese (optional)	2 tbl

1. Preheat oven to 450°F (230°C). Place sliced potatoes in a bowl and sprinkle with salt, pepper, and oil. Toss well to coat evenly. Place on lightly oiled baking sheet and roast until lightly browned (about 10 minutes).

2. Spread Pesto over pizza crust. Place roasted potatoes on top. Sprinkle Parmesan cheese over potatoes, if used. Bake until dough is lightly browned (about 15 minutes). Serve hot.

Serves 8.
Each serving: cal 147, fat 5 g, cal from fat 29%, chol 0 mg

LOW-FAT PIZZA TOPPINGS

A delicious pizza doesn't have to be high in fat if you choose the toppings carefully. Here are some less common options that will add pizazz—not fat—to your next pizza: roasted red peppers (see page 21), sliced zucchini, broccoli florets, sliced artichoke hearts, snow peas, baby corn, sliced eggplant, sliced sweet red onions, jalapeño chiles, water chestnuts.

Pizza con Polenta

Golden polenta is transformed into the hearty crust that makes this vegetarian pizza irresistible.

as needed	olive oil	as needed
2 cups	polenta	500 ml
1 cup	boiling water	250 ml
2	eggs	2
¾ cup	grated mozzarella cheese, part skim milk	175 ml
¼ cup	chopped green onions	60 ml
¼ cup	chopped red bell pepper	60 ml
1 cup	thinly sliced mushrooms	250 ml
2 cups	Sugo di Pomodoro (see recipe on page 50) or bottled pizza sauce	500 ml
1 cup	thickly sliced plum tomatoes	250 ml
¼ cup	chopped Italian parsley	60 ml
1 tbl	minced basil	1 tbl

1. Preheat oven to 450°F (230°C). Lightly oil a 16-inch (40-cm) pizza pan.

2. In a large bowl combine polenta with 1 cup (250 ml) cold water, then add the boiling water in a steady stream, mixing with a whisk. Stir in eggs and mozzarella cheese. Press mixture evenly onto pan. Bake until lightly browned and crisp (10–15 minutes).

3. In a large skillet over medium-high heat, sauté green onions in 1 tablespoon olive oil for 1 minute, then add bell pepper and mushrooms. Cover and let steam for 5 minutes.

4. Spoon sauce over crust, then top with sautéed vegetable mixture, sliced tomatoes, parsley, and basil. Bake until topping is bubbly (12–15 minutes). Serve immediately.

Serves 8.
Each serving: cal 224, fat 7 g, cal from fat 26%, chol 60 mg

FOCACCIA

By most accounts, focaccia is reckoned to be Italy's oldest bread—a simple yeast dough flattened and baked on a stone slab in a wood-fired hearth. Quite likely, it's the grandfather of the famous Neapolitan pizza. Today's cooks can easily make this versatile country bread at home, even without the stone and hearth. Garnished as you like—here, with sautéed onions and basil—focaccia can partner salads and soups, sliced tomatoes and cheese, or cocktails.

1¼ cups	warm water (105°F or 41°C)	300 ml
¾ tsp	sugar	¾ tsp
1 pkg (1 tbl)	active dry yeast	1 pkg (1 tbl)
2¾ cups	unbleached flour	650 ml
as needed	olive oil	as needed
½ cup	minced onion	125 ml
⅓ cup	minced basil	85 ml
1½ tsp	coarse salt	1½ tsp
½ tsp	freshly ground black pepper	½ tsp
as needed	cornmeal, for dusting	as needed

1. Combine ½ cup (125 ml) of the water, the sugar, and yeast in a large bowl. Set aside 10 minutes. Stir in ¾ cup (175 ml) of the flour, cover, and let rise in a warm place 2½ hours.

2. While dough is rising, heat 1 tablespoon oil in a skillet over low heat. Add onion and sauté until onion is soft but not browned (about 15 minutes). Remove from heat and stir in basil, ½ teaspoon of the salt, and pepper.

3. Add the remaining flour to dough and beat well. Combine another tablespoon oil and the remaining warm water, then add to dough. Beat until dough forms a mass. Turn out onto a lightly floured surface and knead until dough is shiny and smooth (about 8–10 minutes). Transfer dough to a lightly oiled bowl and turn to coat all sides with oil. Cover and let rise again until doubled in bulk (about 1½ hours).

4. Preheat oven to 450°F (230°C). Punch dough down and roll into a large rectangle about ½-inch (1.25-cm) thick. Transfer to a baker's peel or baking sheet sprinkled with cornmeal. Spread top with onion mixture. Sprinkle with the remaining coarse salt and bake until golden (about 15 minutes). Cool slightly on a rack. Serve warm.

Makes 1 large flatbread, 8 servings.
Each serving: cal 210, fat 6 g, cal from fat 24%, chol 0 mg

WHOLE WHEAT BREAD STICKS

Bread sticks are a staple of Italian cuisine. This whole wheat version includes a dough that can be shaped in two ways: into plain, straight sticks or more intricate twists. To make twists, roll dough into extra-thin strands and cut into 2 equal lengths, then twist loosely together and pinch ends together to seal.

1 pkg (1 tbl)	active dry yeast	1 pkg (1 tbl)
⅔ cup	warm water	150 ml
	(105–115°F or 41–46°C)	
1 tbl	sugar	1 tbl
½ tsp	salt	½ tsp
as needed	olive oil	as needed
2 cups	unbleached flour	500 ml
½ cup	whole wheat flour	125 ml
1	egg white	1

1. Sprinkle yeast over the water in large bowl of electric mixer. Add sugar. Let stand until yeast is soft (about 5 minutes).

2. Add salt and ¼ cup (60 ml) oil. Add 1½ cups (350 ml) of the unbleached flour; mix to blend. Then beat at medium speed until smooth and elastic (about 5 minutes). Stir in whole wheat flour and about ¼ cup (60 ml) more unbleached flour to make a stiff dough.

3. Turn dough out onto a lightly floured surface coated with some of the remaining unbleached flour. Knead until dough is smooth and satiny and small bubbles form just under surface (about 5 minutes), adding just enough flour to prevent dough from being sticky. Place dough in a lightly oiled bowl and turn to cover all sides with oil. Cover and let rise in a warm place until doubled in bulk (45 minutes– 1 hour).

4. Punch dough down; cover and let rest for 10 minutes. Divide into halves, then cut each half into 18 pieces. Using palms of hands, roll each piece into strands about 8 inches (20 cm) long for sticks or about 16 inches long (40 cm) for twists.

5. Place strands parallel and about ½ inch (1.25 cm) apart on lightly oiled baking sheets. Let rise until strands look puffy (15–20 minutes). Preheat oven to 325°F (160°C). In a small bowl combine egg white and 1 teaspoon water. Brush bread sticks lightly with egg white mixture and bake until crisp and lightly browned (35–40 minutes). Transfer to wire racks to cool.

Makes 36 bread sticks, 18 servings.
Each serving: cal 94, fat 3 g, cal from fat 31%, chol 0 mg

SWEET RED PEPPER LOAVES

Sweet red bell pepper speckles these little loaves of crusty bread and tinges them with a golden color.

as needed	olive oil	as needed
1	red bell pepper, seeded and finely chopped	1
1 pkg (1 tbl)	active dry yeast	1 pkg (1 tbl)
1⅓ cups	warm water	335 ml
	(105–115°F2 or 41–46°C)	
1 tbl	sugar	1 tbl
1½ tsp	salt	1½ tsp
3¾ cups	unbleached flour	850 ml
1 tsp	cornstarch	1 tsp

1. Into a pan over moderate heat pour 2 tablespoons oil. Add red pepper and sauté, stirring often, until soft but not browned (about 5 minutes). Remove from heat and let cool.

2. Sprinkle yeast over ⅓ cup (85 ml) of the warm water in large bowl of electric mixer. Add sugar. Let stand until soft (about 5 minutes). Stir in remaining warm water, red pepper mixture, and salt.

3. Add 2¼ cups (550 ml) of the flour. Mix to blend; then beat at medium speed until smooth and elastic (about 5 minutes). Stir in about 1 cup (250 ml) more flour to make a soft dough.

4. Turn dough out onto a lightly floured surface. Knead until dough is springy and small bubbles form just under surface (20–25 minutes), adding just enough flour to prevent dough from being sticky. Place dough in a lightly oiled bowl and turn to coat all sides with oil. Cover with plastic film; let rise in a warm place until doubled in bulk (about 1 hour).

5. Punch dough down; cover and let rest for 10 minutes. Divide into two equal portions. Shape each into a round ball. Place on lightly oiled baking sheets. Let rise until almost doubled in bulk (30–45 minutes).

6. Preheat oven to 375°F (190°C). In a small pan dissolve cornstarch in ⅓ cup (85 ml) cold water. Bring mixture to a boil over medium-high heat, stirring until thick and clear. Let cool slightly. Brush each loaf with warm cornstarch mixture. With a razor blade cut a large X about ½ inch (1.25 cm) deep at center of each loaf.

7. Bake until loaves are brown and sound hollow when tapped (30–35 minutes). Transfer to wire racks to cool.

Makes 2 small loaves, 6 servings.
Each serving: cal 368, fat 6 g, cal from fat 15%, chol 0 mg

Polenta alla Griglia

Like southern Italy's pasta, northern Italy's polenta is a low-fat staple that can be enjoyed in a variety of ways. Here it is cooled until firm, then sliced and grilled over a charcoal fire. You can also cook it on an indoor griddle or under a broiler.

1½ tsp	coarse salt	1½ tsp
1 cup	polenta	250 ml
1 tbl	olive oil	1 tbl
2 tbl	freshly grated Parmesan cheese	2 tbl

1. In a heavy saucepan bring salt and 4 cups (900 ml) water to a boil. Gradually add polenta, whisking constantly. Cook over low heat, stirring continuously with a wooden spoon, for 20 minutes. Mixture will become quite thick. Stir in olive oil and Parmesan cheese.

2. Pour about a cup of water into an 8-inch (20-cm) loaf pan, tipping to coat inside of pan surface, then drain. Pour polenta into pan. Cool, then chill until firm.

3. Prepare a medium-hot charcoal fire. Slice polenta ½ inch (1.25 cm) thick. Grill on both sides until hot throughout. Serve immediately.

Serves 4.
Each serving: cal 168, fat 5 g, cal from fat 26%, chol 2 mg

LEMON RISOTTO

Arborio rice, spiked with the tartness of lemon, creates a dish that goes well with seafood or poultry.

1 tbl	unsalted butter	1 tbl
1 tbl	olive oil	1 tbl
¼ cup	minced onion	60 ml
2 tsp	grated lemon zest	2 tsp
1½ cups	Arborio rice, washed and drained	350 ml
4½ cups	heated Chicken Stock (see page 30)	1 l
¼ cup	lemon juice	60 ml
¼ cup	freshly grated Parmesan cheese	60 ml
to taste	salt and freshly ground black pepper	to taste

1. In a heavy saucepan over moderately low heat, melt butter and olive oil. Add onion and lemon zest; sauté slowly for 5 minutes. Add rice; stir to coat with oil. Turn up heat to high; sauté rice, stirring, for 30 seconds. Immediately add ½ cup (125 ml) of the stock; reduce heat to medium low and stir until stock is absorbed.

2. Add more stock, ½ cup (125 ml) at a time, stirring constantly and adding more only when previous portion has been absorbed. When all stock is absorbed (about 20–25 minutes), stir in lemon juice. The rice should be tender with a firm center.

3. Stir in Parmesan cheese. Cook over low heat to melt cheese. Season to taste with salt and pepper. Serve immediately in warm bowls.

Serves 4.
Each serving: cal 379, fat 10 g, cal from fat 23%, chol 12 mg

Meat, Poultry, and Fish

Paper-thin slices of beef with herb-scented fresh tomatoes, roasted chicken seasoned with crushed sage and balsamic vinegar, swordfish steaks surrounded by tender chunks of fennel and fresh tomato sauce—these are just some of the tantalizing, low-fat entrées in this section. Included are useful tips for cooking with parchment (see page 73) and selecting low-calorie Italian wines (see page 75).

CARPACCIO

This popular Venetian dish is made with lean raw beef sliced and pounded tissue-thin, then served with a piquant sauce of fresh tomatoes, herbs, and lemon juice.

1 lb	beef tenderloin, trimmed of all fat	450 g
2 lb	fresh tomato, peeled, seeded, and chopped (see page 51)	900 ml
½ cup	minced Italian parsley	125 ml
¼ cup each	minced oregano and basil	60 ml each
⅓ cup	fresh lemon juice	85 ml
½ tbl	freshly grated Parmesan cheese	½ tbl
to taste	salt and freshly ground black pepper	to taste
2 tbl	minced chives (optional)	2 tbl
1 loaf	French bread, sliced thinly	1 loaf

1. Cut beef into 10 thin slices and put each slice between two sheets of plastic wrap or waxed paper. Refrigerate until shortly before time to serve.

2. In a bowl combine tomatoes, parsley, oregano, basil, and 1 tablespoon of lemon juice. Marinate mixture at room temperature for at least 10 minutes or up to 1 hour.

3. Remove beef from refrigerator and pound with a mallet or the bottom of a skillet until beef is paper-thin. Arrange tenderloin slices on individual plates. Scatter tomato mixture around them. Drizzle with remaining lemon juice and dust with Parmesan cheese. Sprinkle with salt and pepper and garnish with chives, if used. Serve with slices of French bread.

Serves 12.
Each serving: cal 232, fat 10 g, cal from fat 39%, chol 27 mg

SCALOPPINE AL LIMONE

The secret of success with this recipe is pounding the veal into very thin slices that will melt in your mouth. Enjoy this low-fat version of a traditional Venetian classic with steamed baby artichokes or Piedmont Pepper Salad (see page 18).

1 lb	veal scallops	450 g
¾ cup	flour	175 ml
2 tsp	salt	2 tsp
1 tsp	white pepper	1 tsp
2 tsp	olive oil	2 tsp
½ cup	fresh lemon juice	125 ml
⅓ cup	minced Italian parsley	85 ml
2 tbl	capers	2 tbl
2 tbl	minced dill	2 tbl
as needed	lemon slices, for garnish	as needed

1. Score the top of each veal scallop with a sharp knife. Place each veal scallop between two layers of waxed paper and pound with a meat mallet until very thin and tender.

2. Mix flour, salt, and pepper on a shallow plate. In a skillet heat oil. Dredge scallops in flour; then lightly sauté them. The scallops will curl and brown when they are done; do not overcook. Place veal scallops in a warming oven.

3. Add lemon juice, parsley, capers, and dill to the skillet and heat for 1 minute, scraping browned bits from bottom.

4. Pour lemon juice mixture over veal and serve, garnished with lemon slices.

Serves 4.
Each serving: cal 238, fat 6 g, cal from fat 21%, chol 95 mg

Pollo Arrosto

Balsamic vinegar adds robust flavor to this herb-infused chicken dish. If you like, you can prepare the dish several hours ahead of time, refrigerate it, and then remove it from the refrigerator about 20 minutes before you are ready to put it in the oven.

1 (3 lb)	roasting chicken	1 (1.4 kg)
2 cloves	garlic	2 cloves
2 tbl	olive oil	2 tbl
1 tbl	minced tarragon	1 tbl
1 tsp	crushed dried sage	1 tsp
6 tbl	balsamic vinegar	6 tbl
6	new potatoes	6
¼ cup	pitted Greek olives	60 ml

1. Preheat oven to 375°F (190°C). Remove skin from chicken. Place chicken in roasting pan, breast side up. Peel and halve garlic cloves, rub surface of chicken with cut garlic, then place cloves inside chicken.

2. Mix together olive oil, tarragon, sage, and vinegar. Rub over surface of chicken and inside cavity. Cut potatoes in quarters and place olives and potatoes around chicken. Cover pan and place in oven.

3. Roast until juice runs clear when a sharp knife is inserted into thigh of bird (45 minutes–1 hour). Slice or cut chicken into serving pieces. Spoon cooking liquid over chicken and serve with olives and potatoes.

Serves 6.
Each serving: cal 190, fat 7 g, cal from fat 34%, chol 25 mg

CHICKEN WITH PROSCIUTTO

These succulent chicken rolls have a surprise in the center—a thin layer of savory prosciutto. Baked in parchment paper to seal in natural juices, these tender bundles produce a scrumptious combination of flavors.

2	whole chicken breasts, boned, halved, and skinned	2
as needed	salt	as needed
2 slices	prosciutto	2 slices
4 leaves	basil, for garnish	4 leaves

1. Preheat oven to 350°F (175°C). Wash breast halves and pat dry. Lightly salt breasts on both sides.

2. Halve prosciutto slices lengthwise. Lay breast halves on a cutting board and cover each with a half-slice of prosciutto. Roll up and tie with kitchen string.

3. Place each roll on a sheet of parchment paper (see page 73). Seal and place parchment packets on a baking sheet. Bake for 35 minutes.

4. Open packets, remove breasts, snip and remove string, and garnish each breast with a basil leaf.

Serves 4.
Each serving: cal 345, fat 11 g, cal from fat 30%, chol 144 mg

CHICKEN AND TOMATOES IN PARCHMENT

This chicken baked in parchment is tender, moist, and fragrant with the aroma of herbs. Parchment paper is available in most supermarkets and is a boon to the health-conscious cook because it allows cooking without extra fat (see opposite page). Packets may be assembled the day before, wrapped in plastic film, and stored in the refrigerator until baking time.

3	whole breasts of chicken, boned, halved, and skinned	3
3 cups	coarsely chopped tomatoes	700 ml
¼ cup	minced shallot	60 ml
1 cup	dry white wine	250 ml
2 tbl	minced tarragon	2 tbl
2 tbl	minced Italian parsley	2 tbl

1. Preheat oven to 375°F (190°C). Following general directions on page 73, lay out 6 sheets of parchment paper on table or counter and place one chicken breast in the center of each. Top each breast with ½ cup (125 ml) tomatoes and 2 teaspoons minced shallot. Add 2–3 tablespoons of white wine to each packet and evenly distribute tarragon and parsley over each breast.

2. Fold the parchment packets as directed on page 73. Place sealed packets on baking sheets and bake for 20 minutes. Serve hot, opening packets carefully to release steam..

Serves 6.
Each serving: cal 182, fat 2 g, cal from fat 11%, chol 65 mg

Parchment Cooking

Cooking in parchment is a popular technique that has two wonderful advantages. First, very little or no fat is required because foods cooked in parchment retain their moisture and flavor. Second, parchment paper replaces the cooking pan, so it reduces cleanup.

Parchment cooking is ideal for foods that have a tendency to dry out when cooked conventionally, such as baked poultry, fish, and vegetables. Fresh herbs, spices, wine, and lemon are all you need to add to make a dish that is low in fat and full of flavor. Follow these easy steps to make parchment packets.

1. Cut a piece of parchment about four times the size of the food item you are cooking. Fold parchment in half. Starting at the fold, cut out a half-heart shape.

2. Open the heart and place the food in the center. Starting at the fold nearest the top of the heart, fold in the edges of the parchment to form an envelope around the food, overlapping the folds as you work your way toward the tip of the heart.

3. Fold the tip of the heart several times to secure. Place packet on a baking sheet and bake according to recipe instructions.

GRILLED SICILIAN CHICKEN

Serve this dish with Pomodori con Zucchine (see page 33) for a healthy and refreshing summertime meal.

1	plump chicken (about 4 lb or 1.8 kg)	1
2	lemons	2
1 tbl	minced garlic	1 tbl
to taste	salt and freshly ground black pepper	to taste
2 tbl	olive oil	2 tbl
as needed	oil, for grill	as needed

1. Prepare charcoal fire for indirect-heat method of cooking (placing a drip pan underneath center of rack, with coals heaped around sides of pan).

2. Wash chicken thoroughly and pat dry. Using a citrus zester or fine grater, remove zest from lemons and set aside. Juice both lemons.

3. Combine lemon zest and juice with garlic, salt, pepper, and olive oil. Coat chicken inside and out with lemon zest mixture, reserving remainder for basting.

4. When coals are covered with a light ash and are no longer flaming, place chicken on lightly oiled grill directly over coals to sear. Sear chicken on all sides, then place over drip pan, breast side up. Close lid. Grill for 1–1½ hours, basting occasionally with reserved basting mixture. Chicken is done when juices run slightly pink to clear, or when an instant-read thermometer reads about 165°F (74°C). Serve hot.

Serves 6.
Each serving: cal 411, fat 14 g, cal from fat 30%, chol 209 mg

PESCE AL LIMONE E VINO

Lemon juice and white wine combine to create a poaching liquid for fish (see photo on page 10). The result is a perfect marriage of flavors. The lemon juice and wine also make a low-fat marinade for grilled fish.

⅓ cup	lemon juice	85 ml
½ cup	dry white wine	125 ml
4	fish fillets	4
2 tbl	minced Italian parsley	2 tbl

1. In a large skillet over medium-high heat, bring lemon juice and wine to a boil. Lower heat to medium. Add fish and cover skillet.

2. Poach fish until it flakes easily when touched with a fork (5–8 minutes). Remove from poaching liquid and serve immediately, sprinkled with parsley.

Serves 4.
Each serving: cal 228, fat 6 g, cal from fat 26%, chol 88 mg

CHOOSING LOW-CALORIE WINES

If you're concerned about the high calories associated with alcohol, here are some guidelines to keep in mind: In general, sweet, full-bodied wines tend to be higher in calories than their dry counterparts. For example, a 3½-oz (105-ml) glass of sweet vermouth, a popular aperitif wine, contains 167 calories, while the same amount of dry vermouth contains only 105 calories. A 3-oz (85-ml) glass of port contains 158 calories, while the same amount of dry red or white wine, such as Soave or Grignolino, contains only 65 calories.

ITALIAN-STYLE SEA BASS

High on flavor and very low in fat, sea bass is wonderful when baked in a savory tomato and pepper sauce. If sea bass is unavailable, try using fillets of perch, flounder, snapper, or turbot.

1 tsp	olive oil	1 tsp
1 clove	garlic, minced	1 clove
¼ cup	seeded and chopped green pepper	60 ml
¼ cup	chopped onion	60 ml
1 can (8 oz)	tomatoes	1 can (225 g)
1 tbl	lemon juice	1 tbl
1 tbl	chopped basil or oregano	1 tbl
4	sea bass fillets	4

1. Preheat oven to 350°F (175°C).

2. In a medium frying pan, heat oil. Add garlic, pepper, and onion and sauté until softened. Add tomatoes (breaking them up with a fork) and their juice, lemon juice, and basil and heat through.

3. Place fillets in a single layer in a shallow baking dish. Pour the tomato mixture over the fish and cover with foil.

4. Bake until fish flakes easily when touched with a fork (15–20 minutes).

Serves 4.
Each serving: cal 140, fat 4 g, cal from fat 24%, chol 47 mg

CALAMARI NAPOLI

This flavorful squid (calamari) dish is good hot or cold.

4 lb	squid, cleaned	1.8 kg
2 tbl	olive oil	2 tbl
4 cloves	garlic, minced	4 cloves
4 cups	crushed tomatoes in purée	900 ml
1 tsp	dried oregano	1 tsp
6	basil leaves	6
to taste	salt and freshly ground black pepper	to taste
¼ cup	chopped Italian parsley	60 ml
1 tsp	hot-pepper flakes	1 tsp

1. Cut squid crosswise into ¾-inch (1.6-cm) rings. Also cut the tentacles if they are large.

2. In a Dutch oven, heat oil. Add squid and sauté for 5–6 minutes. Add garlic and stir for 1 minute.

3. Add tomatoes, oregano, basil, salt, and pepper. Cover and allow to cook until squid are tender (about 20 minutes). Stir in parsley and hot-pepper flakes.

Serves 8.
Each serving: cal 294, fat 7 g, cal from fat 21%, chol 529 mg

A LOW-FAT ALTERNATIVE TO MEAT

As a low-fat, high-protein source, fish is an excellent replacement for high-fat meat entrées. Believe it or not, 3 ounces (85 grams) of flounder contains the same amount of protein as an equal portion of roast beef. Fish is also lower in fat than meat, as well as lower in calories (as long as it is not served with cream sauce or butter). Fish that are particularly low in fat include flounder, sea bass, monkfish, haddock, and sole.

PESCE SPADA AL FORNO

Sicilian cooks know dozens of ways to prepare their prized swordfish (pesce spada). In this classic dish it is baked with tomato sauce, fennel, and herbs.

1 tbl	olive oil	1 tbl
1	onion, diced	1
1 tbl	minced garlic	1 tbl
¼ cup	dry white wine	60 ml
½ cup	chopped basil	125 ml
½ cup	chopped Italian parsley	125 ml
8 small bulbs	whole fennel, trimmed	8 small bulbs
2 cups	Sugo di Pomodoro (see page 50)	500 ml
2 lb	swordfish steaks	900 g
¼ cup	lemon juice	60 ml
to taste	salt and freshly ground black pepper	to taste

1. Preheat oven to 400°F (205°C). Heat oil in a large saucepan over moderate heat. Add onion and garlic and sauté until slightly wilted (about 5 minutes). Add wine, basil, parsley, and fennel. Bring to a boil, reduce heat, and simmer, covered, until the fennel begins to soften (about 10 minutes). Transfer mixture to an ovenproof casserole large enough to hold the fish steaks in one layer.

2. Add tomato sauce to casserole and stir to blend. Arrange fish steaks atop the sauce and pour the lemon juice over fish. Bake until fish just flakes when touched with a fork and fennel is tender (about 20 minutes). Remove fish and fennel to a warmed serving platter. Taste sauce and adjust seasoning with salt and pepper. Spoon sauce over fish and serve immediately.

Serves 6.
Each serving: cal 377, fat 12 g, cal from fat 27%, chol 62 mg

NEAPOLITAN SEAFOOD STEW

Shellfish soups made in Naples are usually loaded with mussels and clams. This version also includes lean white fish—halibut, haddock, pollack, red snapper, whiting, bass, flounder, or cod.

1 bottle (8 oz)	clam juice	1 bottle (225 g)
1 tsp	dried thyme	1 tsp
¼ tsp	fennel seed, crushed	60 ml
1	bay leaf	1
½ lb	lean white fish	225 g
12	prawns, shelled and deveined, or mussels or clams, scrubbed	12
1	tomato, seeded and chopped (see page 51)	1
to taste	salt and freshly ground pepper	to taste
as needed	finely chopped parsley, for garnish	as needed

1. In a large saucepan over high heat, combine clam juice, thyme, fennel seed, bay leaf, and 2 cups (500 ml) water. Bring to a boil.

2. Reduce heat, cover, and simmer for 3 minutes.

3. Cut fish into 1-inch (2.5-cm) chunks. Add fish, shellfish, and tomato to broth. Gently simmer 3–5 minutes until fish is opaque (mussels and clams will open and prawns will turn pinkish and opaque).

4. Remove bay leaf. Season to taste with salt and pepper. Ladle soup into serving bowls. Garnish with parsley.

Serves 4.
Each serving: cal 124, fat 2 g, cal from fat 17%, chol 77 mg

DESSERTS AND PICK-ME-UPS

Luscious, refreshing, and perfect after meals or anytime you want a little boost, sweets are an essential part of Italian cuisine. The recipes in the following section are low in fat and calories, so you can enjoy them with a clear conscience.

BERRY SORBETTO

Any fruit that yields a good deal of pulp when puréed may be substituted for the raspberries. Other berries, peaches, pears, plums, and melons all give excellent results.

⅔ cup	sugar	150 ml
2 pints	fresh raspberries	900 ml
	or 12 oz (350 g) frozen raspberries,	
	without syrup	
½	lemon, juiced	½

1. In a saucepan over high heat, cook sugar and ⅓ cup (85 ml) water, stirring constantly, until sugar dissolves and mixture reaches a full, rolling boil.

2. Immediately remove from heat and cool to room temperature. Strain through a fine sieve into a jar or bowl. Cover and refrigerate until needed. Sugar mixture should always be well cooled (to about 40°F or 4°C) before being used.

3. Wash and drain raspberries, crush, and put through a sieve or food mill to remove seeds. Remove pulp from mill and place in food processor with sugar mixture and lemon juice. Process until well mixed.

4. Transfer to an ice cream machine and freeze according to manufacturer's instructions.

Makes about 1 quart (900 ml), 4 servings.
Each serving: cal 175, fat 0 g, cal from fat 3%, chol 0 mg

GRANITA CAFÉ

Use freshly ground coffee beans for the best results.

¾ cup	sugar	175 ml
1	cinnamon stick	1
2–3 strips	lemon peel	2–3 strips
2–3	whole cloves	2–3
3 cups	espresso or double-strength coffee, chilled	700 ml

1. In a saucepan combine 1 cup (250 ml) water with all ingredients except espresso. Bring to a boil, stirring constantly until sugar dissolves. Reduce heat and simmer without stirring for 4 minutes.

2. Remove from heat; discard cinnamon stick, lemon peel, and cloves. Cool to room temperature. Stir in espresso. Pour into a shallow pan and place in freezer.

3. Freeze until firm (1½–2 hours), stirring well every 30 minutes. Allow to warm slightly and stir one final time before serving.

Makes about 1 quart (900 ml), 4 servings.
Each serving: cal 164, fat 1 g, cal from fat 4%, chol 0 mg

GRANITA ITALIANA

One of Italy's most popular refreshments, granita is a grainy-textured ice that is best served slightly thawed and slushy. Unlike gelato or sorbetto, granita is frozen without constant churning. Here's a low-sugar version that's delicious and easy to prepare: Purée 2 cups of fresh orange or red grapefruit sections with 1 tablespoon maple syrup and 1 teaspoon lemon juice. Freeze the purée until slushy, then blend briefly in a blender. Swirl into wine glasses for serving.

Granita di Melone

This wonderful low-fat version of granita features melon and lemon. Note that the melon must marinate at least 2 hours, and the blended mixture must chill for another 2 hours.

2 lb	ripe melon (honeydew, cantaloupe, or Persian)	900 kg
⅓ cup	sugar	85 ml
as needed	lemon juice	as needed
2 tsp	grated lemon zest	2 tsp
¼ tsp	freshly ground black pepper (optional)	¼ tsp
pinch each	ground nutmeg and allspice	pinch each
½ cup	diced melon, for garnish	125 ml
as needed	mint sprigs, for garnish	as needed

1. Peel melons, halve, and seed. Cut into chunks and put in stainless steel, glass, or ceramic bowl. Add sugar, 1½ tablespoons of lemon juice, lemon zest, pepper (if used), nutmeg, and allspice. Cover and marinate at room temperature for 2 hours, or refrigerate up to 12 hours.

2. Strain the accumulated juices into a small saucepan. Bring to a boil over high heat and cook 1 minute. Remove from heat and let cool. Combine marinated melon and reduced juices in a food processor or blender and blend until smooth. Chill for 2 hours.

3. Sprinkle 2 tablespoons of lemon juice over diced melon and set aside. Pour melon-sugar mixture into container of an ice cream freezer and freeze according to manufacturer's directions. Serve garnished with diced melon and fresh mint.

Serves 6.
Each serving: cal 104, fat 0 mg, cal from fat 1%, chol 0 mg

STRAWBERRY STRATA

Strata means "layers," in this case layers of tender angel food cake, refreshing ice milk, and icy berries.

1 pkg (12 oz)	frozen raspberries in syrup, thawed	1 pkg (350 g)
to taste	superfine sugar and lemon juice	to taste
1	angel food cake	1
½ cup	kirsch or orange-flavored liqueur	125 ml
1 quart	strawberry ice milk, softened	900 ml
1 quart	fresh strawberries, sliced or chopped	900 ml
½ cup	light whipping cream	125 ml
⅓ cup	sliced almonds, toasted	85 ml

1. Strain raspberries and their syrup through a sieve to remove the seeds. Add sugar and lemon juice to taste to purée and mix well. Refrigerate until needed.

2. Slice cake into ½-inch-thick (1.25-cm) pieces. Cut each piece diagonally to make 2 triangles. Brush both sides of each triangle with kirsch.

3. In a 9- by 13-inch (22.5- by 32.5-cm) freezerproof clear glass dish, lay down a layer of moistened cake slices. Top with enough ice milk to cover cake completely and reach edge of dish. Scatter berries over ice milk. Continue layering with cake, ice milk, and berries, ending with a layer of ice milk topped with berries. (You should have 9 layers in all.) Cover well and freeze until firm. In a small bowl whip the cream. Before serving cake, garnish with whipped cream and toasted almonds. Serve with puréed raspberries.

Serves 10.
Each serving: cal 524, fat 9 g, cal from fat 16%, chol 21 mg

STRATA VARIATIONS

Here are some luscious, simple-to-make variations on Strawberry Strata. Simply substitute the ingredients indicated for those in the recipe on page 86.

Apricot Strata Use vanilla ice milk in place of strawberry, apricot brandy in place of kirsch, and coarsely chopped apricots in place of strawberries. Serve with puréed raspberries, if desired.

Banana Strata Use banana ice milk in place of strawberry, dark rum in place of kirsch, and a combination of rum-soaked raisins and walnuts in place of strawberries. Serve with puréed raspberries, if desired.

Dark Chocolate Strata Use dark chocolate ice milk in place of strawberry, orange-flavored liqueur in place of kirsch, and raspberries in place of strawberries. Serve with puréed raspberries, if desired.

Peach Strata Use peach ice milk in place of strawberry, amaretto in place of kirsch, and coarsely chopped peaches in place of strawberries. Serve with puréed raspberries, if desired.

Pineapple Strata Use vanilla ice milk in place of strawberry, cognac in place of kirsch, and fresh pineapple chunks in place of strawberries. Serve with puréed raspberries, if desired.

ITALIAN HAZELNUT MERINGUES

These crisp meringue cookies studded with toasted hazelnuts and candied orange peel are an excellent accompaniment to red wine. Be sure to toast the nuts for added flavor.

¾ cup	unblanched hazelnuts	175 ml
4	egg whites	4
¼ tsp	cream of tartar	¼ tsp
⅛ tsp	ground nutmeg	⅛ tsp
1 cup	sugar	250 ml
1 tsp	Marsala	1 tsp
2 tbl	finely chopped candied orange peel	2 tbl

1. Preheat oven to 350°F (175°C). Spread hazelnuts in a shallow pan. Bake until lightly browned (8–10 minutes). After removing nuts from oven, reduce temperature to 300°F (150°C). Let nuts cool slightly, then rub off and discard most of the brown skins. Chop nuts finely and set aside. Line baking sheets with parchment paper.

2. In a mixing bowl combine egg whites, cream of tartar, and nutmeg. Beat at high speed until foamy. Gradually add sugar, beating until mixture is stiff and glossy. Beat in Marsala. Blend in hazelnuts and orange peel.

3. Drop by rounded teaspoons, placed about 2 inches (5 cm) apart, onto parchment paper-lined baking sheets. Bake until cookies feel firm when touched lightly in the center (25–30 minutes). Remove to wire racks to cool.

Makes about sixty 2-inch (5-cm) cookies, 60 servings.
Each serving: cal 25, fat 1 g, cal from fat 32%, chol 0 mg

ITALIAN WAFER COOKIES

Made in a special gridded iron called a pizzelle, these cookies can be left flat or rolled into cylinders while hot.

as needed	canola oil, for pizzelle	as needed
1	egg	1
2	egg whites	2
½ cup	sugar	125 ml
2 tbl	canola oil	2 tbl
1 tsp	vanilla extract	1 tsp
1½ tsp	anise seed	1½ tsp
3 tbl	brandy	3 tbl
¼ tsp	salt	¼ tsp
⅔ cup	flour	150 ml

1. Lightly brush grids of iron with oil; preheat iron according to the manufacturer's instructions.

2. In a large bowl whisk egg, egg whites, and sugar until light; add oil and whisk until well blended. Add vanilla, anise seed, brandy, ⅓ cup (85 ml) water, and salt; blend well. Add flour and whisk until just blended.

3. When iron is hot, drop batter by tablespoons onto grids to make a neat, thin circle. (For best results make no more than 2 wafers at a time.) Close lid and bake until browned (45–60 seconds).

4. Remove cookies from grids with a knife and leave flat or immediately use your fingers to roll each cookie into a cylinder about 1 inch (2.5 cm) in diameter. Place cookies seam-side down on a wire rack until cool and crisp.

Makes about twenty-four 4-inch cookies, 24 servings.
Each serving: cal 48, fat 1 g, cal from fat 29%, chol 9 mg

Biscotti di Frutta

Favorites for dunking, biscotti come in dozens of varieties. This version includes anise seed and candied cherries.

2½ cups	flour	600 ml
1½ tsp	baking powder	1½ tsp
¼ tsp	salt	¼ tsp
¼ tsp	anise seed, coarsely crushed	¼ tsp
2 tbl	butter, softened	2 tbl
1 cup	sugar	250 ml
1 tsp	vanilla extract	1 tsp
2 tsp	grated orange zest	2 tsp
3	eggs	3
¾ cup	unblanched whole almonds	175 ml
½ cup	mixed candied fruit	125 ml
¼ cup	candied red cherries	60 ml
as needed	coarse sugar	as needed

1. In a medium bowl stir together flour, baking powder, salt, and anise seed to combine thoroughly; set aside.

2. In a large bowl combine butter and sugar; beat until well mixed. Blend in vanilla and orange zest. Separate 1 egg, reserving white in a small bowl. To butter mixture add egg yolk, then remaining 2 eggs, one at a time, beating well after each addition.

3. Gradually beat in flour mixture until dough is smooth and well blended. Divide dough in half and enclose each portion in plastic film. Refrigerate until firm (about 1 hour).

4. While dough is chilling, combine almonds, mixed candied fruit, and candied cherries.

5. Preheat oven to 350°F (175°C). On a lightly floured surface, roll out 1 portion of dough to an 8- by 12-inch (20- by 30-cm) rectangle. Sprinkle with half of fruit mixture. Starting with a 12-inch (30-cm) edge, roll rectangle compactly, jelly-roll style. Pinch edge and ends to seal. Place, sealed

side down, on a lightly oiled baking sheet. Repeat with other portion of dough.

6. Beat reserved egg white until slightly bubbly; brush egg white over each roll. Sprinkle rolls lightly with coarse sugar. Bake until golden brown (35–40 minutes). Let rolls cool on baking sheet on a wire rack for about 5 minutes.

7. Transfer rolls to a board; with a serrated knife cut rolls on the diagonal into ½-inch (1.25-cm) slices. Place slices, cut sides down, on baking sheets and return to oven. Bake until crisply toasted (15–20 minutes). Transfer to wire racks to cool completely.

Makes about 48 cookies, 48 servings.
Each serving: cal 67, fat 2 g, cal from fat 27%, chol 15 mg

Pesche al Vino

In Tuscany the local red wine is used to marinate sliced peaches, producing a simple and supremely refreshing summer dessert. Choose a young and inexpensive Chianti and ripe peaches that are fragrant but not overly soft.

8	freestone peaches, ripe but firm	8
2 tbl	lemon juice	2 tbl
3 tbl	sugar	3 tbl
3¼ cups	Chianti	750 ml

1. Peel peaches and slice into eighths. Place in a stainless steel, glass, or ceramic bowl. Add lemon and sugar and mix gently but thoroughly. Let stand 5 minutes.

2. Pour wine over peaches and cover. Refrigerate 8 hours or overnight.

3. To serve arrange peach segments in wine glasses or wide-mouthed dessert glasses and spoon a little wine into each glass.

Serves 8.
Each serving: cal 352, fat 0 mg, cal from fat 1%, chol 0 mg

INDEX